OMA and ME
Oma Comes Home For Christmas

By Cherry Charleston Harris
Illustrated by Jason Velazquez

Oma and Me

Oma Comes Home For Christmas

© 2022 by Cherry Charleston Harris

Illustrated by Jason Velazquez

All rights reserved solely by the author. The author guarantees all contents are original and do not infringe upon the legal rights of any other person or work. No part of this book may be reproduced in any form without the permission of the author. The views expressed in this book are not necessarily those of the publisher.

Printed in the United States of America.

ISBN-13: 978-1-7379864-6-1

Cherry Books

It was the month of December, my favorite time of year.
I was so excited because Christmas would soon be here.

Another special joy, the best gift I could receive.
Oma was coming to our house, this year on Christmas Eve.

We decorated our tree with lights and a star so bright

I counted the days one by one on my calendar every night.

On December 23rd, I called my Oma on the phone.

How happy I was in the morning when I looked out the door.

Oma was driving up;
I didn't have to wait any more.

I ran out to her car and jumped up in her arms.

Oma brought me presents.
She had one for Mommy too.

I pointed to our tree and said,
"Look, we too have one for you."

My Mommy read the Christmas story
as the two of us sat quietly.

I learned about the little baby
that the shepherds came to see.

Oh, what a special holiday; one that I will never forget.
Oma came to visit us; the best Christmas present yet.

Say it in German

 Christmas: Weihnachten (vai-ee-knock-ten)

 Star: Der Stern (dare stairn)

 Christmas tree: Der Weihnachtsbaum (dare vai-ee-knocks-balm)

 Gift: Das Geschenk (dahs guh-shank)

 toys: Das Spielzeug (dahs sp-eel-zo-eg)

www.ingramcontent.com/pod-product-compliance
Lightning Source LLC
Chambersburg PA
CBHW051332110526
44590CB00032B/4493